PORTRAIT PAINTING
FROM ROMAN EGYPT

PORTRAIT PAINTING FROM ROMAN EGYPT

BY

A. F. SHORE

PUBLISHED BY

THE TRUSTEES OF THE BRITISH MUSEUM

LONDON

1972

First published 1962
Revised edition 1972

SBN 7141 0917 7

Printed in Great Britain
at the University Press, Oxford
by Vivian Ridler
Printer to the University

CONTENTS

INTRODUCTORY NOTE

The portraits which form the subject of this handbook are exhibited in the galleries of the Department of Egyptian Antiquities. Those still attached to mummies will be found in the First Egyptian Room, the others, in the Coptic Gallery. The latter include portraits deposited on permanent loan by the Trustees of the National Gallery, by whose kind permission plates 2, 4–5, 6, 8–16 are reproduced here.

In the course of the preparation of the handbook I greatly benefited from the helpful criticism of Professor John Harris of Copenhagen University and Professor Klaus Parlasca of the Friedrich-Alexander Universität, Erlangen-Nürnberg. I also profited from a discussion with Mr John Keen, formerly Museum Assistant in the Department of Egyptian Antiquities, of his own experiments of painting in a wax medium. To them, to my colleagues Dr I. E. S. Edwards and Mr T. G. H. James and to all with whom I have had the opportunity of discussing the portraits, I would express my grateful thanks.

A. F. Shore

PORTRAIT PAINTING FROM ROMAN EGYPT

The portraits of men, women and children on wood or canvas found with mummies from cemeteries of the Roman Period in Egypt are among the more notable antiquities from an age which – in Egypt at least – is scarcely distinguished for the quality of its art. They represent almost our only surviving body of material for the study of ancient portrait painting. The best of the portraits are remarkably well pre-served and the eye is immediately caught by the rich and luminous quality of the paint. So far removed are they from the conventions of Pharaonic art in the method of reflecting light and of marking shade, that they seem to belong to our own age. This striking modern look of the portraits and the strong human interest of their subject matter make a direct and immediate impact.

At the time of their first appearance, in the first half of the first century A.D. two generations or so had passed since the incorporation of Egypt as a province of the Roman Empire following the defeat and suicide of Cleopatra VII in 30 B.C. The Macedonian Dynasty of the Ptolemies, of which Cleopatra was the last representative, had ruled Egypt for close on three hundred years. This was not the first time that Egypt had come under foreign domination but whereas previously these periods of alien rule had not fundamentally altered the peculiar character of the Pharaonic civilization, now under the Ptolemies the traditional isolation of the country and the long continuity of its uniform culture was effectively broken; land and people were drawn firmly into the world of the Eastern Mediterranean. The story of Egypt from this time is as much the concern of the classical student as the Egyptologist and the many objects of every-day life and funerary use recovered from Roman Egypt occupy a sort of limbo in museum collections, uncertain whether their proper place is with a department of Egyptian or Classical antiquities.

THE RECOVERY AND PROVENANCE
OF THE PORTRAITS

The first examples of portraits to reach Europe were those still attached to mummies brought from the Saqqara necropolis in 1615 by Pietro della Valle, a Roman of noble birth who was one of the first Europeans of modern times to travel extensively in the Near East. The earliest examples acquired by the Museum are three portraits of boys from the collections formed by Henry Salt, British Vice-Consul in Egypt at the beginning of the last century. Two are painted on the mummy wrapping and the third is on a thin wooden panel originally attached to the mummy. They are of archaeological interest rather than of artistic merit. Six other portraits from the Salt collection were acquired by the Louvre and are said to have been found together in association with the burial of Soter, archon at Thebes in the time of the emperor Hadrian (A.D. 117–138). Part of the same find, including the well-known inner coffin of Soter decorated with a large representation of the goddess Nut surrounded by the twelve signs of the zodiac, is now in the Museum. The half of another panel painting, that of a young girl, was acquired from the sale of the collection of the antiquities of Joseph Sams in 1834.

One of the Salt portraits, that of the young man on the wood panel, was noted by Thomas Pettigrew in his *History of Mummies* (London, 1836); the engraving of the portrait which he gives is the first coloured reproduction of any portrait. In spite of the importance of the portraits, as Pettigrew realized, for the study of the ancient technique of painting in wax, which had been widely discussed on the basis of the literary evidence of classical authors from the time of the Italian Renaissance, it was not until the publication of *L'Encaustique et les autres procédés de peinture chez les anciens* by Cros and Henri in 1884 that the available material was properly assembled and investigated. By that time the Museum had enriched its collection of mummy portraits by the acquisition in 1856 of a wooden panel containing the portrait of a young lady of particular interest since it is said to have come from Saqqara (pl. 7).

The appearance of the study by Cros and Henri was timely; within a few years of its publication the number of portraits available for study was greatly increased by two remarkable finds in the region of El-Faiyum, an area rich in agricultural land where intensive reclamation schemes were put in hand during the Ptolemaic and Roman Periods for the settlement of veterans.

In 1887 and subsequent years the Viennese antiquarian and dealer, Theodor Graf, acquired about 300 portraits and fragments said to have come from Er-Rubiyyat on the north eastern side of El-Faiyum, a burial ground used by the inhabitants of Philadelphia, a township established in the Second Century B.C. and named after Arsinoe Philadelphus. It is, however, probable that more than one cemetery was ransacked by Graf's agents. Some ninety of these portraits were exhibited in Europe and America and are described in several editions of a sale catalogue, the most exhaustive being that of Buberl published in 1922. The remainder of the Graf collection (which does not appear in the catalogues) was sold from 1930 onwards by the heirs of Graf. The Graf portraits are now widely dispersed throughout museums and private collections. The Museum's collection includes eight from this source, presented or bequeathed by the late Sir Robert Mond.

The second of the great finds was made by Sir Flinders Petrie in the course of excavations conducted by him in 1888 and again in 1911, in El-Faiyum at the Roman cemetery of Hawara which lies to the north of the great pyramid of Ammenemes III and the site of the ancient 'labyrinth'. Here were buried the inhabitants of Arsinoe (Crocodilopolis), one of the chief centres of El-Faiyum. These excavations resulted in the recovery of 146 mummies with portraits, including some of the finest from the point of view of artistic merit and state of preservation. From Petrie's excavations come the sixteen examples deposited since 1936 on permanent loan by the Trustees of the National Gallery and three others, still attached to the mummies, including that of Artemidorus, presented to the Museum by Martyn Kennard Esq, in 1888 (see pls. 1 and 19).

Since the greater number of examples have come from El-Faiyum, the paintings are frequently referred to as 'Faiyumic portraits', though in fact they have been found in a number of sites from Saqqara in the north to Aswan at the southern frontier of Egypt. But the only other site comparable with El-Faiyum for the quantity and quality of the portraits is Antinoopolis (Antinoe), the city founded by the emperor Hadrian on the occasion of his visit to Egypt in A.D. 130 in memory of his favourite Antinous, accidentally drowned in the Nile at that point. These portraits were recovered in excavations between 1896 and 1911 by the French archaeologist Albert Jean Gayet.

The association of the portraits from Antinoopolis with the emperor Hadrian (A.D. 117–138) provides one of the few circumstantial indications for the dating of the portraits. Fragments of papyri found in one or two cases with the mummies are of Roman date. There is similarity between mummy portraits and portraiture at Pompeii which was destroyed in A.D. 79. No portraits have been found in cemeteries of a purely Ptolemaic character. In spite of earlier claims of a Ptolemaic date for some of the portraits—including a perverse attempt to identify individual portraits with members of the Ptolemaic royal family—internal evidence provides no support for any dating before the Roman Period.

The most useful criteria for the dating of the portraits are the hairstyle and beards of the men and the coiffure and jewellery of the women. Dress, technique and style give additional valuable indications.

In hairstyles the portraits show the influence of the fashions set by the imperial family at Rome and made familiar by statues of the emperors which were set up in the provinces. The variety of styles depicted in the portraits suggests that changes of fashion at Rome were assiduously copied in Egypt, probably with no great lapse of time. Though there may be doubt about the placing of individual portraits, particularly in the case of children or of youths and young girls where it might be expected there was less consciousness of the world of fashion, it is clear that the earliest of the surviving portraits date from the first half of the first century A.D., that the majority fall in the second and third centuries, and that perhaps a quarter of the total number belong to the fourth century. The discontinuance of them after this time is connected with the gradual abandonment of mummification in favour of simple interment of the dead in their everyday clothes, a change accelerated by the rapid spread of Christianity through the villages of Egypt during the third and fourth centuries.

HAIRSTYLE, JEWELLERY AND DRESS

The earliest portraits of men show the same simplicity of hair arrangement and severity of features as stone busts of the late Claudian and Flavian Periods. It reflects the taste and style of the Roman Republic rather than the Hellenistic world. The men have short straight hair arranged in a neatly combed fringe across the forehead. They are usually clean-shaven or with merely the vestige of a growth, as if shaving was not a daily habit. The style is well illustrated by the two portraits on pls. 5 and 6.

The number of portraits which can be assigned to the pre-Hadrianic Period is relatively small. The apparent increase in portraits during the second century may perhaps be explained by the chance of discovery and the accident of preservation. It is however likely that the visit of Hadrian to Egypt in A.D. 130 and the general impetus which it gave in Egypt to the intellectual life of the municipalities encouraged the patronage of the portrait painters.

In style the second century portraits of men are characterized by an elaboration and ostentation which is in marked contrast with the simplicity and severity of the preceding century. Following the fashion set by Hadrian himself and continued throughout the Antonine Period, the men are usually shown with luxuriant curly hair and curly beards. It might convey an air of foppery (pl. 9), or of philosophic studiousness (pl. 10).

The earliest portraits of women show the same simplicity, if not severity, of the pre-Hadrianic male portraits. They are graceful, charming, and feminine. One of the best portraits of this style is illustrated on pl. 2. The neat curls across the forehead and the two plaits falling behind the ears are reminiscent of stone busts of the imperial household in the later part of the Claudian Period, about the time of the emperor Nero (A.D. 54–68). In the later part of the first century the portraits of women begin to show the elaboration of hair arrangement which became a stock theme for the Roman satirist. It was usual to part the hair horizontally across the crown of the head. The back hair was braided and coiled two or three times on the top of the head, while the front hair was arranged in an elaborate series of short curls. These fashions are characteristic of the Flavian Period (A.D. 69–117) and continue throughout the second century. Typical examples are on pls. 11 and 12.

Portraits which can be assigned to the third century with certainty on the evidence of the hair-style are less common and may reflect the general impoverishment of the Roman world, in part political and in part economic, before the reforms of Diocletian (A.D. 284–305). Conditions in Egypt were aggravated by invasion and occupation. There was a fashion at this time among men for close-cropped heads with short curls and trimmed beards or clean-shaven chins. The style was made popular by Caracalla (A.D. 211–217) whose statues in Egypt represent some of the latest of Egyptian sculpture in the monumental tradition. It is best illustrated in the collection by the portrait of a man with a coarse and brutal cast of features (pl. 16).

The return to more normal conditions in the fourth century is reflected in an apparent increased production of portraits. After the division of the Roman world in A.D. 313, Egypt belonged to the Eastern half of the empire ruled from Byzantium. Some male portraits show similarity in the arrangement of hair, in the carefully groomed moustaches and beards and in their general physiognomy to imperial busts of Constantine (A.D. 313–337) and his immediate successors (pl. 4). But in general the resemblance between the portraits of this century and the stone busts is less well marked, as a more native idiom emerges.

The women are almost always depicted with necklaces and ear-rings. Throughout the whole series of portraits this jewellery is with very few exceptions derived from models current in the Hellenistic world and scarcely reflects the typically Egyptian amulets and figurines of gods. Material remains from Egypt show that there is little true native jewellery found after the turn of the era.

In the earlier portraits the style of jewellery is in keeping with the simplicity of the hair-styles. The most common form of necklace is a single gold chain from which is suspended a crescent-shaped amuletic pendant the exact significance of which is unknown (pl. 2). It is not peculiar to Egypt and is found still in use in portraits of the fourth century (pl. 18).

During the second century two necklaces are usual, occasionally three or four are found. One might be a gold chain or a string with gold beads. The other necklace, or both, might be made up of semi-precious stones, many of which were readily obtainable from the desert confines of Egypt; green for beryls, red for carnelian, garnets and perhaps also for rubies, white for pearls, and blue for amethyst, lapislazuli and turquoise. The range of stones is more extensive than it had been in Pharaonic Egypt, when the beryl mines around Sikeit on the Red Sea coast were unworked and rubies and pearls were not known. Also in fashion during the second century are large oblong plaques of opaque glass, coloured in imitation of precious stones, enclosed within a gold mount.

In the later portraits the jewellery is often carelessly painted; two strings remain usual. Large medallions with a precious stone and framed in a gold mount come into fashion.

Three types of ear-rings are found and no woman is depicted without one of them; they are also sometimes found on portraits of young boys. In the earlier series of portraits the most popular form of ear-ring is in the shape of a large gold disk or spherical ball, a type which continues in use to the fourth century when it tends to become larger, rounder and clumsier. It is quite common in the second century but a more popular type during this century is in the form of a thin hoop of gold set with two or three stones. A bar-type of ear-ring, in the form of a cross-piece from which two or three vertical pendants are suspended, seems to have been less in general favour but it occurs in both early and late portraits; two pendants are usual in the earlier portraits, three in the later.

In cases where the portraits include the bust and arms, it is usual for the women to wear bracelets of gold or silver, twisted in the shape of a snake, on both wrists.

Compared with the constant changing of fashions in hair-styles and to a less marked degree the variation in the display of jewellery, the mode of dress is more consistent. Throughout the period of the portraits men and women are shown wearing the ordinary costume of daily life current throughout the Hellenistic world. It consisted of a simple tunic, usually of linen but later also of wool, coming over both shoulders. It was normally woven in one piece, with a central opening for the head and two projecting sleeves. The back, front, and arm-pieces were sewn together at the edges, producing a loose sack-like garment. Two such tunics were usually worn and the under-tunic is sometimes indicated showing above the neckline of the second tunic in later portraits and very occasionally also in earlier ones.

In many of the later examples this tunic alone is shown but in portraits of the first and second century it was customary for men and women to be depicted with a loose garment (*pallium*) over the tunic, draped over either shoulder or wrapped around both.

With male portraits the normal colour of this costume was white or white with a grey or green tint. In portraits of women the colour is usually a deep rich red, less often violet; blue, green and white are also found. The tunic was decorated with two narrow vertical bands running over the shoulder on either side (*clavi*) which in the eastern Mediterranean had no significance of rank. During the first and second centuries the shoulder bands are usually shown as black in colour edged with gold. Red is also common and is more usual in the later portraits, though purple, green, and blue are also found. In fourth century portraits, and sometimes earlier, woven ornamentation occurs on the bands, being indicated by horizontal white strokes or points across the *clavi*. There is also a tendency in the fourth century and occasionally earlier for a coloured border to be added to the neckline of the tunic which is modishly cut back to a point instead of the simple contour of a half-circle.

Less common than the representation of the everyday costume are the portraits of men wearing the Greek *chlamys*, an outer garment fastened over the left shoulder and hanging in loose folds. It is not common until the third century and may indicate the holder of a municipal office. The profession of the soldier is sometimes indicated by the wearing of the *sagum*, a blue cloak, and *balteus*, a leather belt ornamented with gold and silver round buckles worn across the chest and over the left shoulder. Occasionally men are shown with undraped shoulders; in such cases the intention may be to represent the dead man in the prime of his youth as a young gymnast. The bearded man, illustrated on pl. 8, has on his forehead a seven-pointed gold star, indicating that he held a priesthood of the sun-god, identified in Egypt with Serapis. It occurs also on other portraits.

THE PEOPLE AND THE PERIOD

There is little information of a personal nature concerning the various individuals depicted in the portraits. Only in a few cases do we know their names or professions. Where the portrait has been preserved still attached to the mummy, the name may be written on the mummy case, on the bandages or on some object found in close association with the burial in Greek or in the native demotic script. Exceptionally the name may be painted in Greek in white on the background of the portrait and in one early case the name and affiliation are given in the demotic script across the neck of the portrait. The few names which have survived are for the most part names of Greek origin, like that of Artemidorus, inscribed in gold leaf lettering on the mummy case to which the portrait is still attached (pl. 19). His name is followed by a valediction characteristic of burials of the Roman period, 'Farewell' written in Greek.

PLATE I. *Portrait of Artemidorus painted in encaustic on thin wooden panel still attached to the mummy case (see plate 19). A gold wreath has been painted across the hair and another has been added around the top of the panel with a cross-like design in the centre. The lower part of the panel is framed by a row of gold studs. The two gold hawks' heads are the terminals of a floral necklace which is part of the normal Pharaonic decoration of a mummy case.*
From Hawara. Early IInd Century A.D. (B.M. 21810, Presented by H. Martyn Kennard, Esq., 1888).

PLATE 2. *Portrait of a young woman painted in encaustic on thin panel in an impressionist manner. The portrait is one of the earliest and one of the finest of the Hawara series, showing great mastery in the handling of light and shade. The hair is arranged in small tight curls across the forehead and two plaits fall behind the ears to the shoulders, a style fashionable during the late Claudian Period. The jewellery consists of a gold chain with gold crescent-shaped pendant and gold ball-type earrings, the reflecting light being marked by two blobs of white wax on the yellow background.*
From Hawara. Middle 1st Century A.D. (N.G. 2914).

There is no certain example of the name of a profession being added. Painted in white on the canvas shroud of the mummy of a young woman called Hermione of the first century A.D. is the Greek word *grammatike*, 'scholar' or perhaps 'teacher of letters'.

Though as individuals the subjects of the portraits are for the most part anonymous, as a group they form a recognizable element in the society of Roman Egypt. It is clear from the portraits themselves, from their date and provenance, and from the style of dress and display of jewellery, that these people were from well-to-do Hellenised families whose way of life is familiar from Greek papyri recovered in thousands from the sands of Egypt. Racially they were a cosmopolitan group. Some no doubt were recent settlers in Egypt, veterans of the legions which had taken part in the civil wars terminating the Roman Republic. Now disbanded, they had settled in Egypt with their families as cleruchs, that is to say as hereditary holders of agricultural land granted as a gratuity for their service. Other families would have been able to trace their descent back to Greek, Macedonian and other racially mixed but Hellenised immigrants who had come to find employment in Egypt, as administrators, soldiers, merchants and bankers in the wake of the invasion of Alexander the Great in 331 B.C. and the subsequent establishment of the Ptolemaic Dynasty by the Macedonian general, Ptolemy, son of Lagos.

These immigrants settled not only in the Greek-style municipalities founded by the Ptolemies but also throughout the length of the Nile Valley. At the time of the incorporation of Egypt as a province of the Roman Empire, they could no longer be thought of as foreigners. They were an established group of the settled population of Egypt. They themselves certainly thought of Egypt as their homeland. If they no longer represented the dominant force that they had been in Egyptian life during the rule of the Ptolemies, their numbers and ability were sufficient for the Roman administration to classify them as a separate and privileged entity, readily distinguishable from the old indigenous population not so much by virtue of their racial antecedents as by their mode of speech and education.

The vast majority of the old Egyptian families, still the largest element in the population, were employed on the working of the land and continued to be subjected to a life of constant toil and lack of ease. The Hellenistic enclaves enjoyed a privileged position. It was from them that the Romans recruited their administrators.

The privileged and protected status of this group, its loyalty to Hellenistic traditions and natural belief in its intellectual superiority, ensured the survival of the Hellenistic culture in Egypt. The native culture during the first two centuries still found vigorous expression. In Upper Egypt, for instance, the great sandstone temples at Denderah and Esna, Kom Ombo and Phyle were completed in Roman times and the emperors are depicted in relief on the walls, clothed in the traditional regalia of the pharaohs with their names carved in the hieroglyphic script, the last so represented being the emperor Decius in the middle of the third century. Surviving copies of literary texts in demotic, a cursive script for writing the indigenous language on papyrus, are dated for the most part to the first two centuries A.D. Nearly all the categories found in the literature of the Pharaonic Period are represented.

To judge from the vast quantity of Greek literary fragments from Egypt, translations of this native literature in the demotic script on papyrus, or of ritual and mythological texts inscribed in hieroglyphs on temple walls, were not published in Greek. It may be doubted whether many of these Hellenised families of the portraits were truly bilingual: ability to read the native script, written without vowels by means of an unsystematic combination of phonetic and non-phonetic signs, would have been rare. The barrier of script was probably the greatest single factor preventing a true fusion of the native and Hellenistic cultures.

Where the two cultures merge is in the sphere of popular religion and funerary practice. These Hellenised families spoke and wrote in Greek, but they intermarried with the old Egyptian families and adopted Egyptian style names. They honoured the Egyptian gods, in particular those deities who were considered as healers and saviours, as the numerous terracotta figurines used as votive offerings or household images show with their mixture of Greek and Egyptian elements. They adopted the age-old pharaonic practice of mummification and with it the beliefs of Egyptian origin concerning the after-life and the necessity of the preservation and protection of the dead body. The elaborate decoration of the mummies – the portraits, the plaster and canvas head-pieces, the painted burial shrouds, painted wooden coffins and carton-nage cases – show a mixture of Egyptian elements and Hellenistic adaptations. Here in this popular mass-produced hybrid art where the two streams of inspiration clash rather than coalesce, one must seek the origin of the distinctive and uniform culture which emerges in the fourth century and finds characteristic expression in the stone-work, textiles and frescoes of the Coptic period. The ancient Egyptian contribution to Coptic iconography is small and with the exception of the *ankh*-cross not readily apparent. The Hellenistic contribution is subtlely transformed: it is not the least merit of the portraits, executed at first in a style and technique which derives from classical sources, and preserved as a result of the use to which they were put in accordance to ancient pharaonic beliefs, that this transformation can best be demonstrated by analysis of the change of style between the earlier and later series.

STYLE OF THE PORTRAITS

There is no example of true portrait painting for direct comparison from Ancient Egypt; but in the painting which has survived in the tombs, the human figure is almost invariably drawn with the face in profile. Occasionally and only in minor figures of the composition is a face drawn frontally. Colour is applied flatly and attempts at rendering light and shade, depth and perspective are rudimentary; the religious and funerary purpose underlying the paintings did not make for startling innovation and experiment.

The earlier series of mummy portraits are drawn with the face turned slightly to the left or right or sometimes frontally. They are never drawn in profile. Head, shoulders and the upper part of the breast are usually shown and in later examples painted directly on the canvas enveloping the mummy the full figure might be painted. Only occasionally and usually in the later series of portraits are the hands and arms depicted holding perhaps a wreath of red flowers or a drinking cup of glass, symbols of funerary significance.

In the earlier portraits, gradations of the individual colours, the use of shading and high lights, the modelled relief-like effect of the features and the brilliance of the colours give the portraits depth and perspective. At close quarters the work looks casual, almost rough and coarse. One is conscious of the brown eyes with the enlarged black pupils, the prominent dark line of the eyebrows, the white streak down the nose, the thick red smear of the lips separated by a black line and the heavy shading under the chin. But at a distance of three or four feet these prominent features merge and blend with the background and the effect is that of living individual persons momentarily caught as their head turns in recognition at the call of a friend. This suggestion of movement in the pose and this impressionistic handling of the paint shows the influence of classical tradition and is not of native inspiration.

In the later examples, the portraits are more stylised. The figures are almost invariably full faced: the drawing is less assured; the mouth is represented with a shut, pursed underlip drawn with an exaggerated bow. The hair is arranged in a single mass, lying on top of the head and following its contours as if it were an appendage to, and not part of, the features. But though the realistic drawing of the earlier series gives way to a more formal, geometrically balanced arrangement which tends to suppress the powerful sense of character, nevertheless at its best the style produced some notable examples which will bear comparison with the finest of the earlier portraits. One need only compare the portrait of the lady illustrated on pl. 3 with that on pl. 4. Even the worst daubs have a certain meretricious charm from their superficial resemblance to some contemporary schools of painting.

THE TECHNIQUE OF THE PORTRAITS: TEMPERA AND ENCAUSTIC

Most of the portraits are painted on wooden panels: a smaller number of both early and late portraits are executed on the linen shroud enveloping the corpse. This latter method is more common with children than with adults. No examples of panel painting have survived from ancient Egypt, though in the sixth dynasty tomb of Mereruka at Saqqara (about 2300 B.C.) there is a representation of the deceased using an easel. Examples of painting on the mummy shrouds in the Pharaonic period are so isolated that it may be said that there was no native tradition for it.

In the earlier panels the wood is usually a thin slice of cypress, imported probably from Syria. The thickness of the panel is no more than $\frac{1}{16}$ of an inch or so; the height is usually about 17 inches and the width about 9 inches. The panels are roughly trimmed to a point or arch at the top and were placed with few exceptions with the grain of the wood running vertically over the face of the mummy and secured in position beneath the bandages. Thicker panels, about $\frac{1}{4}$ inch in thickness are more usual in the later period. These are generally rectangular in shape measuring on an average 12 inches in height and 8–9 inches in breadth. Native woods seem to have been used, like sycamore; lime, which, though not indigenous to Egypt, was introduced during the Hellenistic period, was also employed.

The paint might be applied directly onto wood or canvas. It was, however – at least in the case of the wooden panels – more usual to prepare a ground of gypsum plaster which might be white or a shade of grey according to the impurities present in the gypsum which occurs plentifully in Egypt in a natural state. This background might also be tinted by use of coarsely ground pigment mixed in with the plaster. A plaster consisting of an admixture of whiting (chalk) and glue was also used. Both preparations are loosely referred to as 'gesso' in Egyptological literature and are familiar from the Pharaonic period. On this quick-drying, firm, smooth base the portrait would first be roughly sketched out in black, or more rarely red, outline before the paint was applied.

The pigments consist in the main of naturally occurring mineral earths and artificially prepared mineral compounds, long familiar in Egypt and readily obtainable from local sources. Black pigment is a finely ground carbon which might be acquired in different forms as soot or lamp black or powdered charcoal. Yellow and red were prepared from ochres, naturally occurring earths in which the colouring is due to the presence of iron compounds. Red lead was also used, a preparation probably introduced into Egypt during the Roman period. The principal source of blue pigment is frit, a crystalline compound which can be artificially prepared by heating together silica (sand or quartz pebbles), a copper compound (usually malachite) and calcium carbonate (if not already present in the sand). The pigment was widely used in the Hellenistic and Roman world and the writings of classical authors such as Vitruvius recognize its Egyptian origin. In Egypt from the Pharaonic period blue was also prepared from ground azurite and yellow from orpiment. The former is a copper compound obtainable from Sinai and the Eastern Desert, the latter a naturally occurring arsenical compound probably imported. Analysis of specimens has also shown the use of vegetable dyes in the preparation of pigment, like madder, a red dye extracted from certain vegetable roots which was mixed in a chalk or gypsum base.

Two distinct vehicles were used as the medium for the paint. In a number of cases, particularly during the fourth century, the pigments were mixed in water with the addition of an adhesive material. For the latter glue, gum from the acacia tree and egg white were all familiar in the classical world. Though there is no definite confirmation by analysis the probability is that egg white was the normal adhesive. This technique is usual for portraits on canvas.

Portraits executed in tempera have a characteristic freshness and delicacy of colour which is the more remarkable considering their survival over the centuries (pl. 4). Water-colours are easily damaged and the pigment affected by moisture or the action of the air unless the painting is varnished. In some cases the portraits painted in tempera were protected by a thin coat of bees-wax applied over the painted surface. This method had apparently been used in Egypt for a short time in the earlier part of the eighteenth dynasty (around 1500 B.C.) on tempera wall paintings of some Theban tombs, in place of the normal varnish, the exact identity of which is uncertain. It was however far more usual in the case of the mummy portraits for the pigment to be coarsely ground and mixed in with the wax. The process resulted not only in a more robust portrait but in a luminosity and enrichment of colour reminiscent of modern oil painting.

The use of wax as a paint medium does not seem to have been native to Egypt. The technique was apparently introduced from the Hellenistic world where it was widely practised. The various modes of its use in the classical world are described by Pliny the Elder in his *Natural History*, Book XXXV. In his discussion Pliny uses the term 'encaustic' still commonly but perhaps misleadingly applied to the technique of the wax portraits if by that term we are to understand that the whole portrait was achieved by some technique of fusing cold wax to the surface of the panel by the subsequent application of artificial heat. Until the recovery of the mummy portraits, the untidy and literary account of Pliny was the most important source for the study and attempted reconstruction of the ancient technique. The mummy portraits in wax represent almost the total surviving body of actual illustrative material.

Examination of the surviving portraits, study of Pliny's account, and modern experiments with wax have not succeeded in resolving all the problems raised in connexion with the ancient technique. There is still considerable doubt about the manner in which the wax was prepared for the mixing of the pigments and about the mode of its transfer from the paint pot to the painting ground.

The simplest suggestion is that the bees-wax was purified by heating and used without the admixture of any other substance apart from the pigment. There would be little reason for rejecting this suggestion if it were not for the fact that laboratory analysis of the wax has in some cases given a higher melting point than the known melting point of bees-wax. It is uncertain whether this high melting point is due to possible chemical instability of bees-wax over the centuries, to the presence of untraced elements (resin for instance) or merely to the presence of the pigment in its coarsely ground state.

The employment of wax in an emulsified form would satisfactorily account for the high melting point. A wax emulsion can be formed by boiling the wax in water with the admixture of a small quantity of soda which in the form of natron was easily obtained and commonly used in Egypt from an early period. Recent infra-red spectrographical examination has confirmed the presence of soda in both wax and tempera portraits. The emulsification of the wax is a process which might naturally have suggested itself from the purification of the wax, a necessary preliminary to its use as a paint medium. The boiling of yellow bees-wax in sea water with the addition of a little 'nitrum' (that is the natron of Egypt) is described by Pliny as the formula for the making of 'punic wax'. The whitest part is skimmed off, poured into a jar with cold water, reboiled with sea water and then left exposed to the light of the sun and the moon. In the full context the passage seems to be describing no more than a bleaching and refining process to produce the best quality wax; but Pliny's formula for 'punic wax' has been claimed as a description of the making of a wax emulsion and cited as support for the theory of its use in the preparation of the pigments for the wax portraits.

Examination of the portraits clearly shows the use of a brush (probably made from palm fibre) for the application of paint to the background, the drapery, and the hair. In the warm climate of Egypt there is no practical difficulty in applying the wax thinly and evenly over the painting ground with free running strokes of a full brush, provided the work is rapidly executed. A particularly good example of the brushwork is to be seen in the lower part of the portrait of a woman from Hawara (pl. 11), where at the end of a long full sweeping stroke of purple colour for the drapery are the marks of the individual fibres of the brush splayed out flat on the panel.

Some portraits are wholly painted in wax with the brush, but in most

23

cases, in contrast with the freely painted background, hair and drapery, the colour of the flesh tones is laid on in a thicker and creamier state in a manner which has produced a characteristic irregular ridging effect. It is, for instance, particularly noticeable on the portrait of the man illustrated on pl. 5. In some cases the eyelashes are only indicated by scratches as if by a sharp tool. It is frequently suggested and supported by enlarged details of the portraits that in the painting of the features use was made of an instrument called by Pliny the *cauterium*, a word originally used for a branding iron and applied also to a surgical instrument used for cauterizing. It has been claimed that the *cauterium* was a kind of metal spatula or palette knife and that coloured sticks of cold wax were worked on and subsequently fused on to the panel by the application of a heated metal tool of this kind. The irregular nature of the ridging, however magnified by photography, is not proof that a metal tool similar to a modern palette knife was used, for this would have produced a cleaner line.

More plausibly the *cauterium* of Pliny has been identified with long-handled spoon-like bronze instruments found among artist equipment in a late Romano-Gallic tomb at St. Médard in the south of France in 1845-6. From the bowl of the warmed spoon the coloured wax might have been ladled and modelled on the panel. No instrument like the St. Médard *cauterium*, if that is in fact what it is, has as yet been identified from Egypt, in spite of the wealth of everyday objects recovered from tombs and town sites of Ptolemaic and Roman Egypt.

How much weight should be attached to Pliny's account of the *cauterium* so far as the mummy portraits are concerned, is doubtful. It is obvious that in all portraits the brush was the principal tool. No portrait is executed without some evidence of the use of the brush or several brushes of differing thicknesses. There is also evidence in some portraits that the panel was vertical or nearly vertical when the painting was done, as is shown by the downward trickle of blobs of paint in the portrait of a man illustrated in pl. 16. If this is so, it is difficult to see how the *cauterium* was used. It may well be that the attempt to explain or illustrate Pliny's account of the use of the *cauterium* with reference to the mummy portraits from Egypt is misplaced, and that the whole of the painting was done by the brush. The characteristic effect to be seen on the features of the portraits which suggests the use of an instrument other than the brush is consistent with the working of the wax in a creamy state with a hard blunt point, the most likely object so used

24

PLATE 3. *Portrait of a woman painted in encaustic on thick panel. It is one of the latest portraits painted in that technique and forms an instructive contrast with the previous plate. The hair is symmetrically arranged in curls on either side of a central parting. The jewellery consists of a single gold chain with large gold medallion and a pair of bar-type ear-rings with three pendants. The neckline of the tunic has an edging of white and the two vertical bands have woven ornamentation indicated in white at the top.*

From El-Faiyum (Graf Collection). IVth Century A.D. (B.M. 65344, Bequeathed by Sir Robert Mond, 1939).

PLATE 4. *Portrait of a man painted in tempera on a thick panel. The hair, moustache and beard have parallels in imperial portraiture of the Constantine Period. The portrait is one of the best of the later series, though the paint is carelessly applied; the grey of the background intrudes below the line marking the shoulders and there is a streak of grey down the left shoulder.*
From El-Faiyum (Graf Collection). IVth Century A.D. (B.M. 63397, Presented by Sir Robert Mond, 1931).

being a brush stiffened by constant use or the brush end; or the characteristic ridging might well result from the congealing of the wax as it rapidly cooled after repeated application with a brush over the same area. Such explanations have the virtue of simplicity and imply a more uniform and coherent technique which conforms to the general impression of the portraits, that they were rapidly turned out at no great expense.

THE PURPOSE OF THE PORTRAITS

Although in style and technique the portraits belong to the Hellenistic world, the use to which they were put derives its inspiration from ancient Egyptian practice and belief. The portrait was an integral part of the mummy. The funerary purpose may account for the youthfulness of the subjects and the look of calm and serene repose. This is how one wished to remember the dead. In some cases a laurel crown in gilt, symbolizing their future happy state, has been added to portraits of both men and women (pls. 1, 7 and front cover). The jewellery of women may be also added in this way (pl. 7). Sometimes in the Hawara portraits, the wooden panels have been given a gilt stucco border with a pattern of entwining vine leaves in raised relief (pl. 10).

The practice of mummification was developed in Egypt during the Old Kingdom (perhaps as early as 2800 B.C.) as a means of preserving the body. Protection of the body from both decay and disturbance was held to be necessary for the well-being and happiness of the individual personality after death. The origin of the belief may be sought in the predynastic period (before 3100 B.C.). It would have been observed that a corpse buried in a shallow grave in close contact with the sand or gravel of the desert in the hot and dry climate of Upper Egypt was indefinitely preserved as a result of the natural desiccation of the body. Throughout Egyptian history, mummification was the proper and desired form of burial and it was regularly adopted by various foreign elements which at times intruded and settled in Egypt. The persistence of the practice is to be explained by Egyptian religious beliefs concerning survival. Mummification was hallowed by ancient myth which described how Osiris himself, the chief god of the funerary cult, had been mummified by the jackal-headed god Anubis after Isis, his mother, had gathered together the various parts of his body, dismembered and scattered by his evil brother Seth. The dead man was identified with Osiris. By virtue of the mummification process and of the recitation of the correct spells, he partook of the miraculous benefits of the ceremony performed for Osiris by Anubis. On the pink cartonnage case of Artemidorus (pl. 19), scenes deriving from the myth are depicted in gold leaf beneath the funerary formula 'Artemidorus farewell' written in Greek. The top register shows Anubis performing the mummification; the two divine sisters, Isis and Nephthys, stand mourning at each end of the embalming table. Below, the gods Thoth and Horus perform a ceremony before the sacred emblem of Abydos, the chief cult centre of Osiris. In the lowest register the soul of Artemidorus, conceived of in the form of a bird, is shown alighting at its home, the body of the dead man represented in the attire of Osiris. Though by the Roman period the curative process of mummification seems often to have been indifferently carried out, there is no diminution in the accompanying ritual, and it is from this late period that the most informative Egyptian texts relating to the elaborate ritual which accompanied the curative process of mummification have come.

The survival of the individual personality was closely associated in the Egyptian mind with the preservation of the individual features of the face. For the protection of the head of the mummy head pieces of cartonnage, that is layers of linen and papyrus glued together and stiffened with gesso, moulded and painted in the likeness of the human face, were introduced from the time of the Middle Kingdom (about 2000 B.C.). In theory these masks were intended, like funerary statues, as individual portraits of the deceased. It is however seldom that one feels, even in the case of the gold mask of Tutankhamun or the gold masks from the royal cemetery of the twenty-second dynasty at Tanis, in the presence of an individual portrait. It is not until the Roman period, with the appearance of the portrait panels and the contemporary painted plaster head-pieces, that one has the impression of real likenesses.

In view of the date of the first appearance of these panels and masks, it is probable that the realistic element which makes them true portraits derives from Roman influence, though it is less certain that the paintings have any direct connection with the Roman cult of the *imagines*, the wax images of ancestors placed around the *atrium* or open court of the Roman house.

It was Petrie who first suggested that the mummies, contrary to

Egyptian custom of the Pharaonic period, were placed around the open court of a house like the Roman *imagines*. The theory rests upon deductions from Petrie's careful and acute observations of the conditions of the mummy cases and of the circumstances of burial in the Hawara cemetery.

A cursory glance at the Hawara material will confirm the correctness of Petrie's observations. Plate 13 is an example of the damaged state of some of the portraits at the time of burial. The disfigurement to the right eye is ancient. The damaged stucco of the head-pieces, the caked dirt and flymarks on the portraits, the damaged foot-pieces, children's scribbles and smears on the mummy cases, indicated to Petrie that the mummies, with and without portraits, had stood in the open court of the houses for a considerable period of time exposed to the elements, 'where', as he says, 'children were taught their writing lessons, where the dust settled and occasional rain beat in upon the figures and where in the cleaning of the house the foot-cases were gradually knocked to pieces'.[1]

The circumstances of burial lend some support to this theory. In contrast to the elaborate and costly preparation and decoration of the mummies and mummy cases, the actual interment was simple. The mummies with portraits were usually buried in groups in plain pits dug in the sand and gravel of the desert edge and then refilled with the excavated material. No superstructure marked their final resting place and the absence of visible memorial for the graves, which could be located only by searching the whole cemetery area, is reflected in our ignorance of the names of the dead.

Correct though Petrie's observations are, some doubt may be expressed concerning his inferences. Excavation of Roman town sites does not suggest that the individuals of the portraits lived in the Roman-style house with open *atrium*. There is no literary evidence for the keeping of the mummies in the house. Somewhere, one feels, there would have been mention of so bizarre a custom among late classical authors to whom the religious observances of the inhabitants of Egypt were a never failing source of mockery.

There is however literary evidence for the practice of having portraits in the house and the question naturally arises whether the funerary use to which the portraits were put was secondary. Were the portraits in-

---

[1] *Roman Portraits and Memphis (IV)*. (British School of Archaeology in Egypt and Egyptian Research Account, 1911) page 2.

tended in the first place to be hung in the lifetime of the owner in the living quarters of his house, and only subsequently to be used for funerary purposes? The rough way in which some of the panels from Hawara had been trimmed to a point at the top and the finding of chippings in the bandages of the mummy suggest perhaps that the panels have been adapted for the mummy from portraits executed on square panels and intended in the first place for other use. In one case a much damaged portrait on wood was found at Hawara still attached to a square wooden frame with cord for hanging in much the same style as a modern portrait.[1]

It is unwise to generalize on this question of whether the portraits are painted from life or not. Clearly portraits painted on the canvas shroud of a mummy can only have been painted after death, and it is difficult to believe that portraits on the thicker rectangular panels of the later series, particularly those in which the deceased is shown holding a wreath and glass vessel, were ever intended for other than funerary use, painted in all probability after death. On the other hand the degree of individual characterization of the best portraits of the earlier series, like, for example, the two men illustrated on plates 5 and 6, would strongly suggest a study from life. But when the portraits are seen in bulk, one is struck by a certain sameness in the outline of the long oval-shaped faces and in the proportion of the features and above all in the characteristically enlarged eyes. There is in general an absence of portraits of old people. In nearly every case the subject is portrayed in the prime of youth and beauty. The impression that the portraits give as a whole is that the painter at least from the second century, like the modeller of the plaster masks, simplified the wide range of subjects to a small number of well-defined types still to be observed among the peoples of the Eastern Mediterranean.

The speed at which and the scale on which these portraits were turned out, as well as the social status of the individuals portrayed and the broad similarity of technique and style, suggest the quick sketching of a professional journeyman rather than the studied product of the academician's studio. One is reminded of the art of the itinerant limners calling at the country houses of eighteenth-century England or of the

---

[1] Now in the Department of Greek and Roman Antiquities, Hinks, *Catalogue of the Greek, Etruscan and Roman Paintings and Mosaics in The British Museum*. (The British Museum, 1933) page 56 No. 85 and plate 24.

travelling guilds who flourished in Poland during the seventeenth and eighteenth centuries, painting coffin portraits of local nobility and civic worthies in oils on metal plates. These surviving products of unknown painters in the Faiyum and other centres in Roman Egypt, working to the inherited conventions of the classical world, provide our only glimpse of the great portrait paintings of the ancient world.

SUGGESTIONS FOR FURTHER READING

EZIO ALETTI La Tecnica della Pittura Greca e Romano e l'Encausto. (Rome, 1951.)

ERNST BERGER Beiträge zur Entwicklungs-Geschichte der Maltechnik. I–II. Die Maltechnik des Altertums. (Munich, 1904.)

PAÜL BUBERL Die griechisch-ägyptischen Mumienbildnisse der Sammlung Th. Graf. (Vienna, 1922.)

E. COCHE DE LA FERTÉ Les portraits romano-égyptiens du Louvre. (Éditions des Musées Nationaux, Paris, 1952.)

E. COCHE DE LA FERTÉ La peinture de portraits romano-égyptiens au Musée du Louvre. *Bulletin Trimestriel de la Société Française d'Égyptologie*. No. 13 Juin 1953, pp. 69–78.

HENRI CROS ET CHARLES HENRY L'Encaustique et les autres procédés de peinture chez les anciens. (Paris, 1884.)

ELIZABETH DOW The Medium of Encaustic Painting. *Technical Studies*. (Fogg Art Museum, Harvard University.) Volume V, 1936/37, pp. 3–17.

OTTO DONNER VON RICHTER Appendix in Katalog zu Theodor Graf's Galarie antiker Porträts (1889, subsequent editions 1891, 1903: English edition 1890).

HEINRICH DRERUP Die Datierung der Mumienporträts. (*Studien zur Geschichte und Kultur des Altertums*, XIX 1, Paderborn, 1933.)

GEORG EBERS The Hellenic Portraits from the Fayum. (New York, 1893.)

C. C. EDGAR Graeco-Egyptian Coffins, Masks and Portraits. (*Catalogue général des antiquités égyptiennes du Musée du Caire*, Cairo, 1905.)

C. C. EDGAR On the dating of the Fayum Portraits. *Journal of Hellenic Studies*, XXV, 1905, pp. 225–33.

A. EIBNER Entwicklung und Werkstoffe der Wandmalerie vom Altertum bis zur Neuzeit. (Munich, 1926.)

J. FREL Deux portraits de momie à Prague. *Archiv Orientálni* xx (Diatribae Lexa), 1952, pp. 314–20.

GÜNTER GRIMM Thebanische Mumienporträts? *Archäologischer Anzeiger*, 1971, pp. 246–52.

W. DE GRÜNEISEN Le Portrait, traditions hellénistiques et influences orientales. (Rome, 1911.)

E. GUIMET Les portraits d'Antinoë au Musée Guimet. (Paris, 1912.)

HERMANN KUHN Detection and Identification of Waxes including Punic Wax by Infra-red Spectrography. *Studies in Conservation. The Journal of the International Institute for conservation of Historic and Artistic Works*, Volume 5, No. 2, May, 1960, pp. 71–9.

A. L. LAURIE Greek and Roman Methods of Painting. (Cambridge, 1910.)

A. LUCAS Ancient Egyptian Materials and Industries. (Fourth edition, revised and enlarged by J. R. Harris, London, 1962.)

KLAUS PARLASCA Mumienporträts und verwandte Denkmäler. (Wiesbaden, 1966.)

KLAUS PARLASCA Repertorio d'arte dell'Egitto Greco-Romano a cura di A. Adriani. Serie B vol. 1 (Fondazione Mormino, Sicily, 1969.)

V. PAVLOV Egipetsky portret i–iv vekov. (Moscow, 1967, in Russian.)

V. PAVLOV and R. SHURINOVA Fajumski portret. (Moscow, 1965, in Russian with French and English summaries.)

WILLIAM H. PECK Mummy Portraits from Roman Egypt. (The Detroit Institute of Arts, 1967.)

W. M. FLINDERS PETRIE Hawara Biahmu and Arsinoe. (London, 1889.)

W. M. FLINDERS PETRIE Roman Portraits and Memphis IV. (*Egyptian Research Account and British School of Archaeology in Egypt*, XX, London, 1912.)

W. M. FLINDERS PETRIE The Hawara Portfolio: Paintings of the Roman Age. (*Egyptian Research Account and the British School of Archaeology in Egypt*, XXII, London, 1913.)

E. PFUHL Masterpieces of Greek Drawing and Painting. Translated by J. D. Beazley. (London, 1926, New Edition 1955.)

E. REINACH Les portraits gréco-égyptiens. *Revue archéologique* (Paris, 1914–15), série 4, tome 24, pp. 32–53; série 5, tome 2, pp. 1–36.

W. J. RUSSELL Egyptian Colours in W. M. Flinders Petrie, Medum. (London, 1892.) pp. 44–8.

E. SCHIAVI Il sale della terra, materia pittorica dell'antichità. (Mailand, 1961.)

HANS SCHMID Enkaustik und Fresko auf antiker Grundlage. (Munich, 1926.)

GEORGE STOUT The Restoration of a Fayum Portrait. *Technical Studies*. (Fogg Art Museum, Harvard University.) Volume 1, 1932/33, pp. 82–93.

A. STRELKOV Fajumsky portret. (Moscow, 1936, in Russian.)

MARY HAMILTON SWINDLER Ancient Painting from the Earliest Times to the Period of Christian Art. (New Haven, 1929.)

HILDE ZALOSCER Porträts aus dem Wüstensand. (Vienna-Munich, 1961.)

DORA ZUNTZ Two Styles of Coptic Painting. *Journal of Egyptian Archaeology*, XXI, 1935, pp. 63–7.

PLATE 5. *Portrait of a man painted in encaustic on thin panel. A strip at the bottom and at the top of the panel has been left unpainted. The man is depicted slightly older than usual, shoulders undraped, with deep set eyes and well wrinkled face. The effect of severity is increased by the thick and creamy state in which the paint has been laid on for the flesh tones, achieving a kind of impasto effect. The short straight hair combed down the forehead, the beardless chin, stern cast of the features and lines of the face muscles recall the style of Roman portraits during the Flavian Period (69-117 A.D.).*
From Hawara. End Ist Century A.D. (N.G. 1265).

PLATE 6. *Portrait of a man painted in encaustic on thin panel; a narrow strip of wood at the bottom is unpainted. The face shows great character and individuality in the drawing of the eyelids, in the slant of the eyebrows and in the lines of the neck and face, suggesting the painting is from life. In general effect the portrait readily recalls the physiognomy of the emperor Trajan (98-117 A.D.).*
From Hawara. Early IInd Century A.D. (N.G. 2913).

PLATE 7. *Portrait of a woman painted in encaustic on thin panel. A gold wreath and two gold necklaces have been subsequently added; the upper necklace has petal-shaped pendants and the lower a large medallion now partly destroyed. The ear-rings are of the hoop type set with pearl. The drapery is white. The portrait was acquired in 1856 and is of particular interest, being one of the few in the collection from elsewhere than El-Faiyum.*
Said to be from Saqqara. Middle IInd Century A.D. (B.M. 29772, formerly 5619a).

PLATE 8. *Portrait of a bearded man painted in encaustic on thin panel. On his forehead is a seven-pointed gold star indicating his holding of a priesthood of the sun, worshipped in Egypt in the guise of Serapis. The panel on which the portrait is painted is pierced with holes and grooved on the back, as if it had been originally intended to be used for box-making. The drapery is white with red vertical band. From Hawara. Middle IInd Century A.D. (N.G. 2912).*

PLATE 9. *Portrait of a young man painted in encaustic on thin panel. The thick curly hair and curly beard are characteristic of the Antonine Period (138-161 A.D.). The drapery in white.*
From Hawara. Middle IInd Century A.D. (N.G. 1264).

PLATE 10. *Portrait of a young man painted in encaustic on thin panel. The drapery is white with rose red vertical band. The portrait has been given a gilt stucco border with interlacing vines in raised relief.*
From Hawara. Second Half, IInd Century A.D. (N.G. 1261).

PLATE II. *Portrait of a woman painted in encaustic on thin panel. The lower part of the panel is unpainted and the treatment of the drapery shows the clear sweep of the brush strokes. Her tunic is red, the vertical band being black with a gold edging. The jewellery consists of a gold chain with crescent pendant and two gold ball-type ear-rings. The front hair is arranged in a series of short curls around the forehead half concealing the ears. It is rendered by a series of thick black curly lines over the grey background. The back hair is swept up in a coil.*
From Hawara. Early IInd Century A.D. (N.G. 1270).

PLATE 12. *Portrait of a young woman painted in encaustic on thin panel. The tunic is purple with broad black stripe. The ear-rings are gold hoop type set with three stones, a black one between two pearls. The upper necklace is gold with gold medallion enclosing a green stone. The lower necklace is of alternate red and green stones roughly daubed on. The front hair is arranged in short thick black curls coming down to conceal the ears. The back hair is gathered up in two coils on the top of the head and held in position by a gold pin struck obliquely through the hair. From Hawara. IInd Century A.D. (N.G. 1269).*

PLATE 13. *Portrait of a young lady painted in encaustic on thin panel. The red outer garment is draped over both shoulders and skilfully painted in two tones to represent the light and shade of the elegant drape of the folds. The same careful handling is seen in the jewellery; the upper necklace is of green stones, perhaps beryl, and gold spacers, blobs of white wax on the dark green indicating reflected light. The lower necklace is a gold chain of two intertwining strands. The ear-rings are in the form of a gold hoop with spherical gold pendant, with white wax reflecting the light. The hair is symmetrically parted on either side of a wide central parting, with the edge hair indicated with fine strokes from the mass. The damage to the right eye is ancient.*
From Hawara. IInd Century. (N.G. 1267).

PLATE 14. *Portrait of a young lady painted in encaustic on thin panel. The portrait is painted in the same style as that of the previous plate but with less skill; compare for instance the line of the tunic and the drawing of the right ear. The jewellery is more elaborate. The hoop ear-rings are set with three beryls or emeralds; the upper necklace is of similar oblong shaped beryls separated by gold spacers. The lower necklace consists of a chain of gold and garnet beads with a large beryl medallion with two pearl pendants on gold chain.*
From Hawara. IInd Century. (N.G. 1263).

PLATE 15. *Portrait of a young man painted in encaustic on thin panel. The line and the modelling of the undraped shoulders and neck muscles are well suggested. From Hawara. IInd Century. (N.G. 1268).*

PLATE 16. *Portrait of a man painted in encaustic on thin panel. The lower edge of the panel is unpainted. The white paint of the tunic has been put on roughly and a downward trickle of the paint is to be seen in the lower right hand side, showing that the panel was vertical when the painting was done.*
From Hawara. Early IIIrd Century. (N.G. 3139).

PLATE 17. *Full face portrait of a woman painted in tempera on canvas on a thin gesso ground. The central parting of hair is indicated in gilt and a thin red fillet runs across the upper part of the hair. The jewellery is poorly drawn, and consists of a pair of large ball-type ear-rings and necklace with large medallion. The tunic is green with shoulder bands of black edged with gold. Arms are shown with gold snake-bracelets. The right hand holds a garland of red flowers, the left hand, now destroyed, probably held a cup. The portrait, one of the latest from Hawara, retains much of the style and technique of the earlier series in the firm modelling and in the use of cross-hatching of darker shades.*
From Hawara. IVth Century A.D. (N.G. 1266).

PLATE 18. *Portrait of a young girl painted in tempera on canvas primed with gesso. The jewellery consists of bar-type ear-rings with three pendants and two necklaces, the upper of large oblong stone or glass beads, the lower of gold with crescent-shaped pendant. The right hand holds a glass vessel, a gold snake bracelet on wrist. From analogy with other portraits, the left hand was raised to shoulder level and held a red wreath (compare pl. 17). The tunic is purple with broad black bands edged with gold. The outer garment is indicated over the left shoulder.*
From El-Faiyum (Graf Collection). IVth Century A.D. (B.M. 63395, Presented by Sir Robert Mond).

PLATE 19. *Mummy case and portrait of Artemidorus. For detail of the head see plate 1 (in colour). The mummy case is of stucco stained pink and moulded around the bandages of the mummy. The scenes are modelled in relief and covered in gold leaf. They are drawn from Ancient Egyptian mythology. The mummy case was found in a brick-lined chamber together with two others similarly decorated, belonging to another Artemidorus and to a lady, Thermoutharin.*
From Hawara. Early IInd Century. (B.M. 21810, Presented by H. Martyn Kennard, Esq., 1888).

PLATE 20. *Portrait of a young boy painted in encaustic on thin panel, still attached to the mummy. The elaborate arrangement of the bandages in a geometric pattern with gilt studs is typical of mummies containing portraits at Hawara.*
From Hawara. IInd Century A.D. (B.M. 13595, Presented by H. Martyn Kennard, Esq., 1888).